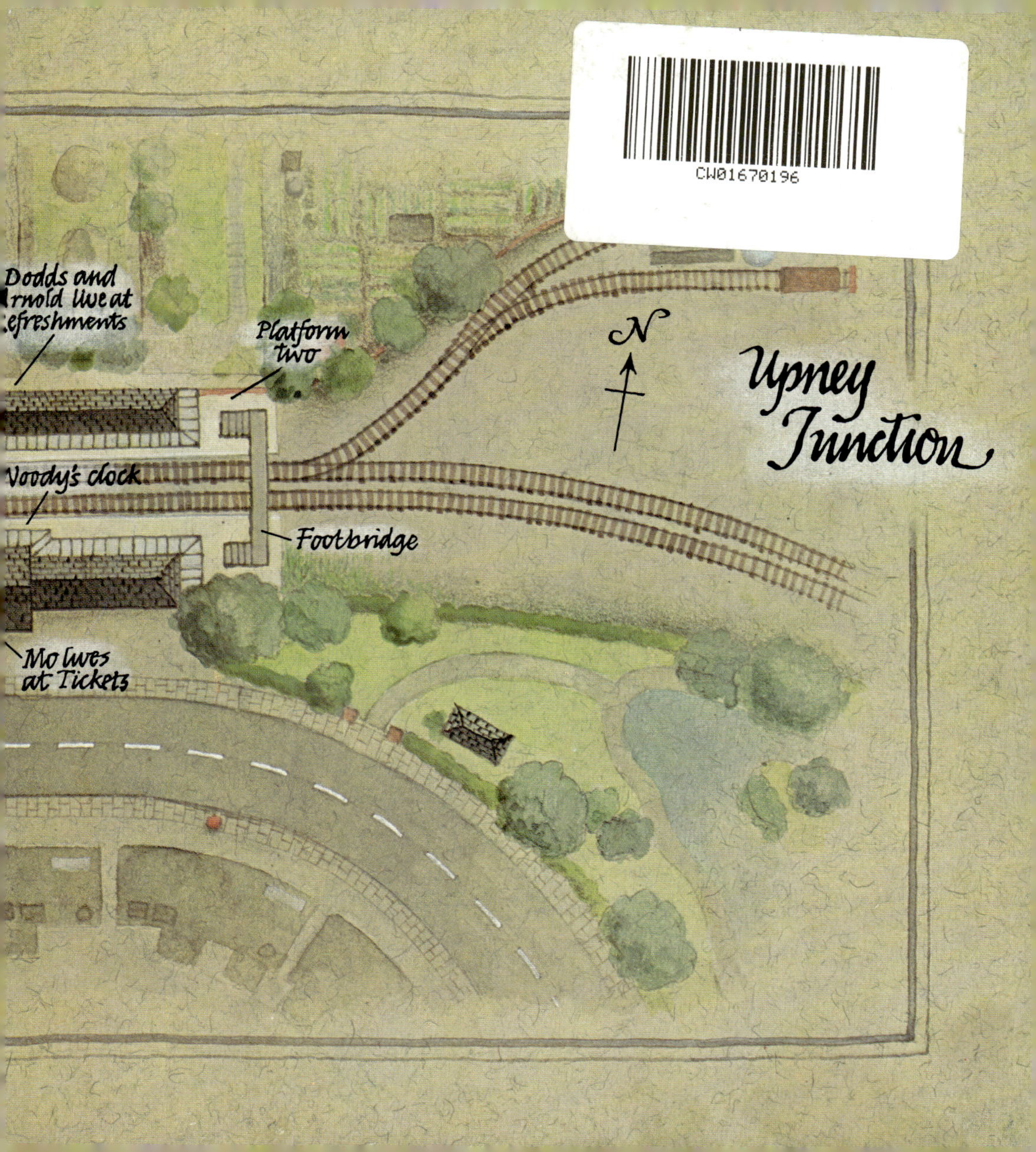

Dodds and
rnold live at
efreshments
Platform
two
Upney
Junction
Voody's clock
Footbridge
Mo lives
at Tickets

Mick, Maurice and Bernard – thanks!

First published 1983 by Macdonald & Co (Publishers) Ltd, Maxwell House, 74 Worship St, London, EC2A 2EN
 ISBN 0 356 09186 4
Printed and bound by Purnell & Sons (Book Production) Ltd, Paulton, England

TREASURE TROVE AT UPNEY JUNCTION

MACDONALD

Woody the mouse was having friends to tea in his clock home above the station manager's office. He and Mo, Dodds and Arnold had just tucked into toasted teacakes and now Dodds snoozed while Arnold watched Woody and Mo playing dominoes. Suddenly the peace was broken by a harsh croak from outside which made them jump and upset the dominoes. Mo went to the door and peered out. On the platform was a strange-looking bird.

'Let's go and see what it wants,' said Mo.

They tumbled out of Woody's clock, down the drainpipe and onto the platform to meet the visitor. When the bird saw them it began to speak loudly.

1

'Roll up, roll up. Your attention please! Bargains galore – from Jack Daw.'

'Hello,' said Mo. 'You're new around here. What are you selling?' The bird beamed.

'Good afternoon gents,' he said. 'Come and 'ave a look. Antiques and high class bric-a-brac – everything to turn a mouse's home into a palace.' The mice gathered round and rummaged through the bird's tray of junk. Woody bought a key for his clock, Mo a whistle and Dodds a toothless comb.

But Arnold wasn't buying. He had seen something he couldn't afford, and he didn't want anything else. It was a beautiful gold medal with a coloured ribbon.

'Ah yes,' said the bird, noticing Arnold. 'Pretty ain't it? It's one of my collection. If you'd like to visit my spacious premises above the clock tower some time I'll show you the lot. But now, if you'll excuse me, I must fly. A pleasure to do business with you.' And with that Jack Daw took off.

That night Arnold couldn't sleep. He was thinking about the medal and longed to see the whole collection. He looked out of the window of Refreshments up to the clock tower.

'First thing tomorrow,' he said to himself, 'I'm going to pay a visit to Mr Jack Daw.'

When the sun rose over Upney Junction, Arnold was already dressed and out on the platform.

'Now,' said Arnold to himself, 'where do I start?'

He began to explore the platform and noticed that one of the pillars supporting the platform canopy was covered with ivy. He put one foot on the thick stem. The climb was under way. Hand over hand he climbed up the creeper until finally he clambered, puffing and blowing, onto the canopy roof.

'Camp one!' he announced triumphantly. 'Where to from here?'

He spotted a rusty drainpipe leading up the station wall. He'd had plenty of practice climbing the pipe that led to Woody's clock, and was soon moving at speed up the inside.

'This is easy,' he thought, as he popped out at the top. Full of confidence, he leapt into the guttering that led to the base of the clock tower, and began to run along it as fast as he could.

'Easy, easy,' he shouted, 'it's . . . . . aieeee!!'

The guttering had given way. Arnold clung to the end for dear life as he found himself swinging through space. Crash! The iron gutter smashed through a dirty window pane taking the little mouse with it.

Arnold lay still for several moments, his eyes shut tight. He felt himself all over.

'No bones broken,' he said shakily, rubbing his eyes. He looked about and saw that he was in a room full of cobwebs and junk. Then he saw it. Pointing the way to the roof, up a steep flight of stairs, was an old, dusty sign. Someone had stuck another notice over the top of the sign. *Jack Daw's Antiques* it read.

Arnold picked himself up off the floor and made for the foot of the stairs. Taking a deep breath he began to climb the stairs one at a time. At the top was a small door. Arnold squeezed through a gap in its rotten frame into a dark space on the other side.

He shivered. What was that strange, musty smell?

'I don't like this place,' he thought to himself. He could hear a strange, low sound coming from the darkness.

'It sounds like Dodds sleeping in a biscuit tin,' he thought. As his eyes got used to the dark he saw a complicated mass of cogs, springs and levers. Arnold was inside the clock. He stepped onto a large metal cog with teeth like stairs and as he climbed he began to sing.

'Hickory, dickory, dock, the mouse ran up the clock . . .'

Just then a loud, droning snore interrupted his song. He stopped short and looked round anxiously.

Then, to his horror, he saw them. Hanging upside down from every possible ledge was row upon row of bats. Luminous eyes stared at Arnold from all around. Some bats, disturbed by Arnold's singing, had even begun to flap about! Three dropped from a rafter and swooped over his head. Arnold's hair stood on end with fright. Soon the air was thick with bats, getting closer and closer. One of them even brushed its leathery wing against Arnold's shoulder! Ugh!

That was enough. Frantically, he scrambled through the clock looking for escape. It was then that he noticed a stout chain running through a hole in the ceiling. Up he climbed. All around him flapped the angry bats but at last he reached the hole and pulled himself through.

'Phew,' said Arnold, and fainted.

When he opened his eyes, he saw a large black figure standing over him. It spoke.

'Hello, mate! What brings you up here?'

'Jack Daw!' exclaimed Arnold with relief. 'Am I glad to see you! Is this where you keep your junk – er, I mean antiques?'

'That's right, my son,' said the bird, helping Arnold to his feet.

'I climbed the clock tower because I wanted to see your collection of medals but I'm afraid I disturbed the bats on the way up'.

'Never trust anyone who sleeps upside down, I say,' said Jack Daw, 'but if it's medals you want, follow me.'

They squeezed past sagging shelves and bulging boxes filled with every kind of junk imaginable.

'You've got enough here to start a lost property office,' said Arnold. Jack Daw stopped in front of a small glass cabinet and unlocked it.

'This is the real stuff in here. Jewellery, coins, and,' he paused to pull out a velvet-lined drawer, 'medals.'

Arnold whistled at the sight of rows of gold and silver medals each with its own bright ribbon. In the middle was the one he had so admired the day before. Arnold was obviously impressed.

'Not bad, eh?' said the bird. 'But now let me show you a real treasure.' He pulled out a shabby leather box and opened it. Inside was a magnificent jewel-studded gold ring. Arnold gasped.

'Handed down to me from my great-great-grandfather. He lived at the Tower of London – say no more,' explained Jack Daw with a knowing wink.

Arnold didn't know what to say. With trembling fingers he picked up the ring to examine it. But, to his dismay, the ring fell onto the floor and bounced straight through a gap in the floorboards! With a cry, Jack Daw sank down and peered through the gap.

'Lawks!' he squawked.

'Can you see it?' asked Arnold nervously.

'Just about,' said Jack. 'It's dropped right down inside the clock. I don't think I could get to it. I'm not even sure you could, even . . . even if the bats weren't there.'

Arnold fell silent at the mention of the bats. He didn't want to face them again. But he knew what had to be done.

'I lost the ring for you, so I'll get it back,' he said bravely.

'Good boy!' exclaimed Jack Daw, 'but I think we might try a different route this time. Come on, it's time for a flying lesson.' Arnold followed his friend to an open ledge high up in the clock tower. He looked out and gasped.

'I – I can't fly!' he stammered, swaying slightly.

'No, but I can,' said Jack Daw. 'Now hold tight!' Without another word he grasped hold of Arnold and launched out from the ledge. Arnold's head swam as he looked down.

The bird flew down in front of the huge clock face and pointed to where it was cracked and broken.

'In there,' he said. 'I'll fly close and you jump for it.' Arnold didn't have time to be afraid. He jumped and managed to scramble in through the clock face.

It was very hot and stuffy behind the glass and the smell of the sleeping bats made Arnold uneasy.

'Now where's that ring?' he muttered as he squeezed through the workings of the clock.

'Aha!' he exclaimed, 'there it is.' The ring was wedged between a large cog and a lever. Arnold tugged at it but it wouldn't budge. He tried again, but nothing moved. Then, as he gave one last heave, everything seemed to happen at once. The ring jerked free, setting the clock ticking loudly. All around Arnold great cogs started to move. There was a flurry of wings from the shadows. The bats had been disturbed.

'Oh dear,' said Arnold, 'here we go again.' Clutching Jack Daw's ring, he began to pick his way past spinning cogs and jerking levers. The bats were fully roused now.

'I could use a suit of armour to get past that lot,' thought Arnold, as he climbed over a large spring. 'That's it!' he said. 'A suit of armour!'

He went back to the spring, stood it up and squeezed inside.

'Perfect!' he said, making one or two practice hops. Then, like a giant pogo-stick, he bounced past the bewildered bats to the safety of the broken clock face where his friend was waiting.

Arnold thrust the ring through the hole and Jack Daw pulled him to freedom. With his passenger swinging below like a hang-glider, the bird flew back to his home in the top of the tower.

Soon the precious ring was back where it belonged and its rescuers celebrating.

'Well,' said Jack Daw presently, 'I think it's time we got your feet back on the ground.'

Together they made their way back to the open ledge.

'I'm getting to like this,' said Arnold as they took to the air once more.

As they swooped down over the platform Jack Daw began to call loudly.

'Roll up, roll up! Gather round everybody!' Before long, all the residents of Upney Junction were assembled looking puzzled.

'What's going on Jack?' called Mo. 'More bargains?'

'No bargains to offer,' replied the bird. 'Just my sincere thanks to a brave friend.'

Arnold blushed.

'Oh, and this,' added Jack Daw. From an inside pocket he drew out the shining gold medal that Arnold had so much admired, and pinned it on Arnold's chest.

'For bravery,' said Jack Daw. 'No charge.'

The other mice all began to talk at once. But Arnold stood, speechless.

'I think we'd all better go back to Tickets,' said Mo. 'Somebody here's got a lot of explaining to do!'

Woody

Mo

Theo